PowerKids Readers:

The Bilingual Library of the
United States of America™

NEW HAMPSHIRE
NUEVO HAMPSHIRE

JENNIFER WAY

TRADUCCIÓN AL ESPAÑOL: MARÍA CRISTINA BRUSCA

The Rosen Publishing Group's
PowerKids Press™ & **Editorial Buenas Letras**™
New York

Published in 2006 by The Rosen Publishing Group, Inc.
29 East 21st Street, New York, NY 10010

First Edition

Book Design: Albert B. Hanner
Photo Credits: © Kurt Stier/Corbis; pp. 5, 11, Albert B. Hanner; pp. 7, 26, 31 Geoatlas; pp. 9, 30, 31 © David Muench/Corbis; p. 13 Library of Congress; pp. 15, 31 © Ron Watts/Corbis; p. 17 © Bettmann/Corbis; p. 19 © Frank Siteman/Index Stock Imagery; pp. 21, 31 © Darrell Gulin/Corbis; p. 23 © Lee Snider/Photo Images/Corbis; pp. 25, 30 © Joseph Sohm; ChromoSohm Inc./Corbis; p. 30 © Eric and David Hoskins/Corbis; p. 30 © Tim Zurowski/Corbis; p. 31 © Stapleton Collection/Corbis

Library of Congress Cataloging-in-Publication Data

Way, Jennifer.
New Hampshire / Jennifer Way ; traducción al español, María Cristina Brusca.—1st ed.
p. cm. — (The bilingual library of the United States of America) Includes bibliographical references and index.
ISBN 1-4042-3094-7 (library binding)
1. New Hampshire—Juvenile literature. I. Title. II. Series.
F34.3.W39 2006
974.2—dc22
                                                        2005016970

Manufactured in the United States of America

Due to the changing nature of Internet links, Editorial Buenas Letras has developed an online list of Web sites related to the subject of this book. This site is updated regularly. Please use this link to access the list:

http://www.buenasletraslinks.com/ls/newhampshire

Contents

Contenido

Welcome to New Hampshire

New Hampshire is known as the Granite State. It got its nickname because granite is one of the most plentiful rocks in the state.

Bienvenidos a Nuevo Hampshire

Nuevo Hampshire es conocido como el Estado del Granito. Este mote se debe a que el granito es una roca muy abundante en el estado.

New Hampshire Flag and State Seal

Bandera y escudo de Nuevo Hampshire

New Hampshire Geography

New Hampshire is in the northeast of the United States. New Hampshire borders the states of Maine, Massachusetts, and Vermont. It also borders the country of Canada.

Geografía de Nuevo Hampshire

Nuevo Hampshire está en el noreste de los Estados Unidos. Nuevo Hampshire linda con los estados de Maine, Massachusetts y Vermont. También linda con el país de Canadá.

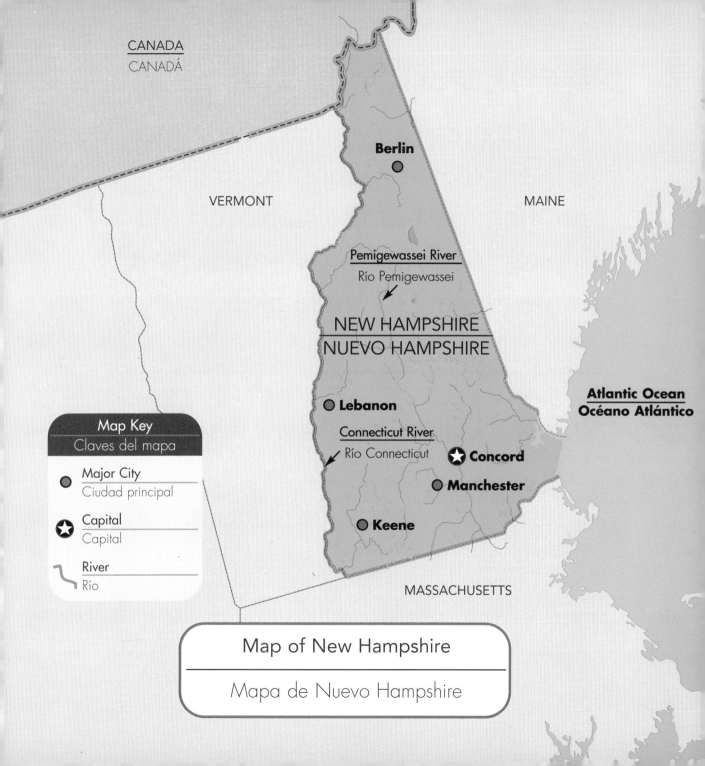

CANADA
CANADÁ

VERMONT

MAINE

Berlin

Pemigewassei River
Río Pemigewassei

NEW HAMPSHIRE
NUEVO HAMPSHIRE

Atlantic Ocean
Océano Atlántico

◉ **Lebanon**

Connecticut River
Río Connecticut

★ **Concord**

◉ **Manchester**

◉ **Keene**

Map Key
Claves del mapa

◉ Major City
Ciudad principal

★ Capital
Capital

River
Río

MASSACHUSETTS

Map of New Hampshire

Mapa de Nuevo Hampshire

New Hampshire has lots of forests and mountains. Mount Washington is in the White Mountains in the northern part of the state. It is the highest peak in New Hampshire. It is 6,288 feet (1,916 m) high.

Nuevo Hampshire tiene muchos bosques y montañas. El monte Washington está en las montañas White, en la parte norte del estado. Es el pico más alto de Nuevo Hampshire. Tiene 6,288 pies (1,916 m) de altura.

Mount Washington

Monte Washington

New Hampshire History

New Hampshire was one of the 13 British colonies. These colonies fought to win their freedom from Great Britain. This was known as the American Revolution, which lasted from 1775 to 1783.

Historia de Nuevo Hampshire

Nuevo Hampshire era una de las 13 Colonias Británicas. Estas colonias lucharon contra Gran Bretaña para obtener su libertad. Esta lucha se conoce como la Guerra de Independencia y duró desde 1775 hasta 1783.

Fort Constitution, an Important Place During the War

El Fuerte Constitution, un lugar importante durante la guerra

John Sullivan was a general in the American Revolution. He was born in Somersworth, New Hampshire, in 1740. One of the important battles he fought in was the Battle of Trenton, in New Jersey.

John Sullivan fue un general de la Guerra de Independencia. Nació en Somersworth, Nuevo Hampshire, en 1740. Una de sus más importantes batallas fue la Batalla de Trenton, en Nueva Jersey.

General John Sullivan

General John Sullivan

Daniel Chester French was born in Exeter, New Hampshire, in 1850. He was a sculptor. His most famous sculpture is of president Abraham Lincoln, at the Lincoln Memorial in Washington, D.C.

Daniel Chester French nació en Exeter, Nuevo Hampshire, en 1850. Chester era escultor. Su escultura más famosa es la del presidente Abraham Lincoln, en el Monumento a Lincoln, en Washington, D.C.

Lincoln Memorial in Washington, D.C.

Monumento a Lincoln en Washington, D.C

Christa McAuliffe was a teacher in Concord, New Hampshire. In 1986, she was chosen to be the first teacher to travel to outer space. She was sent on a spaceship called the *Challenger*. Sadly, the *Challenger* crashed.

En 1986, Christa McAuliffe, una maestra de Concord, Nuevo Hampshire, fue elegida para ser la primera maestra en viajar por el espacio. McAuliffe formó parte de la tripulación de la nave espacial Challenger que, tristemente, estalló.

NASA

Christa McAuliffe

CHRISTA

Living in New Hampshire

In the summer there are fairs throughout New Hampshire. Many people bring to these fairs animals and foods for which the state is known to sell. These foods include jams, cheeses, apples, and maple syrup.

La vida en Nuevo Hampshire

En el verano hay ferias por todo Nuevo Hampshire. Mucha gente lleva los animales y productos por los que el estado es conocido. Estos incluyen mermeladas, quesos, bayas, manzanas, y jarabe de arce (miel de maple).

A Boy and His Calf at the Lancaster Fair

Un chico con su ternero en la Feria de Lancaster

There are many things to do outdoors in New Hampshire. People enjoy skiing, camping, hiking, and biking. In the fall people come to New Hampshire's forests to see the leaves change beautiful colors.

En Nuevo Hampshire hay muchas cosas para hacer al aire libre. La gente disfruta del esquí, los campamentos, las caminatas y el ciclismo. En el otoño la gente viene a los bosques de Nuevo Hampshire para ver el cambio de colores del follaje.

White Mountains National Forest

Bosque Nacional White Mountains

New Hampshire Today

The American Independence Museum is in Exeter. It opened in 1991. Visitors can learn about colonial life and the state's part in American history.

Nuevo Hampshire, hoy

El Museo de la Independencia Americana está en Exeter. Fue inaugurado en 1991. Los visitantes pueden aprender acerca de la vida colonial y sobre el rol del estado en la historia de los Estados Unidos.

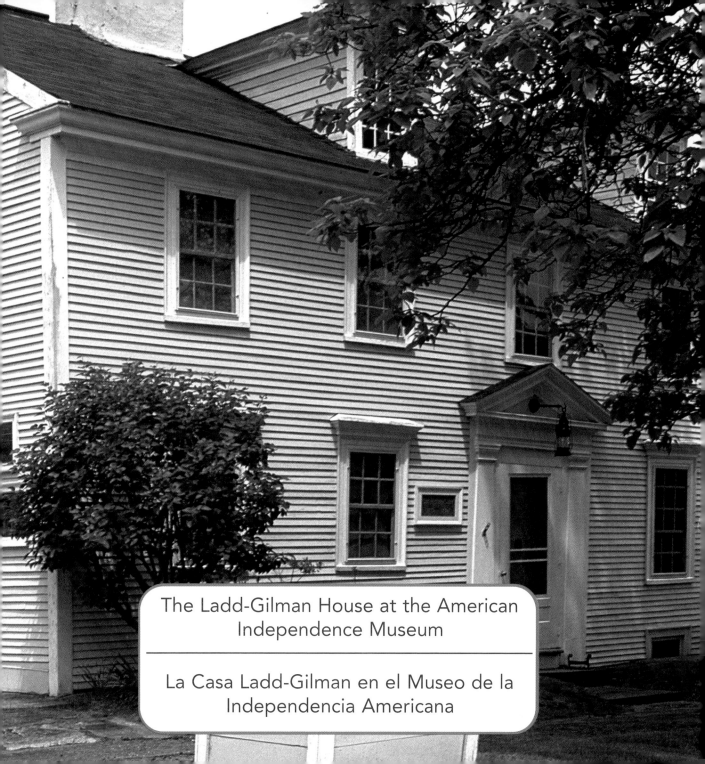

The Ladd-Gilman House at the American Independence Museum

La Casa Ladd-Gilman en el Museo de la Independencia Americana

Manchester, Nashua, and Concord are important cities in New Hampshire. Concord is the capital of the state of New Hampshire.

Manchester, Nashua y Concord son ciudades importantes de Nuevo Hampshire. Concord es la capital del estado de Nuevo Hampshire.

State House in Concord, New Hampshire

Casa de Gobierno en Concord, Nuevo Hampshire

Activity:
Let's draw the Map of New Hampshire

Actividad:
Dibujemos el mapa de Nuevo Hampshire

1

Draw a large rectangle. Add a smaller rectangle on the bottom right.

Dibuja un rectángulo grande. Agrégale un rectángulo pequeño a la derecha de su base.

2

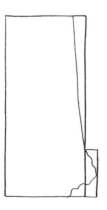

Draw a slanted line down the right side of the large rectangle. Draw a wavy bump inside the small rectangle. Continue the wavy line on the bottom of the big rectangle.

Traza una línea inclinada a lo largo del lado derecho del rectángulo grande. Dibuja un bulto ondulado adentro del rectángulo pequeño. Continúa la línea ondulada adentro del rectángulo grande

3

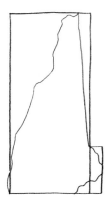

Draw the western side of the state. Use the red line as your guide.

Traza el lado occidental del estado. Usa la línea roja como guía.

4

Add a star for Concord, the capital city. Draw a circle for Manchester, the state's most-populated city. Draw a triangle for Mount Washington. Draw triangles with two vertical lines below them for White Mountain National Forest.

Agrega una estrella en el lugar de Concord, la ciudad capital. Traza un círculo para ubicar Manchester, la ciudad más poblada del estado. Dibuja un triángulo para mostrar el Monte Washington. Dibuja varios triángulos, con dos líneas verticales en su base, para representar el Bosque Nacional White Mountain.

27

Timeline

Cronología

The first permanent English settlement is made at Dover.

1623

Se establece en Dover la primera población inglesa permanente.

New Hampshire becomes a royal British colony.

1679

Nuevo Hampshire se convierte en una colonia de Gran Bretaña.

New Hampshire becomes the ninth state of the Union.

1788

Nuevo Hampshire pasa a ser el noveno estado de la Unión.

Concord becomes the state capital.

1808

Concord llega a ser la capital del estado.

The University of New Hampshire is established.

1923

Se establece la Universidad de Nuevo Hampshire.

The New Hampshire primary becomes the first presidential primary held each election year.

1952

Las elecciones primarias en Nuevo Hampshire se convierten en las primeras elecciones de cada año electoral.

The Old Man of the Mountain, New Hampshire's natural landmark, falls from the top of the mountain.

2003

La famosa roca conocida como el Viejo de la Montaña, cae de la cumbre de una montaña.

New Hampshire Events

Eventos en Nuevo Hampshire

February Frostbite Follies Winter Carnival in Littleton Ice and Snow Festival in Keene	**Febrero** Carnaval de invierno Frostbites Follies, en Littleton Festival del hielo y la nieve, en Keene
May Lilac Festival in Lisbon Chowderfest in Portsmouth	**Mayo** Festival de la lila, en Lisbon Chowderfest, en Portsmouth
June Scottish Games and Celtic Music Festival in Greenfield	**Junio** Festival de música celta y juegos escoceces, en Greenfield
July Canterbury Fair	**Julio** Feria de Canterbury
August Mother Ann Day Umbagog Wildlife Festival, Errol Latino Festival in Manchester Hampton Beach Children's Festival in Hampton	**Agosto** Día de la Madre Ana Festival de la vida silvestre Umbagog Festival latino, en Manchester Festival infantil de Playa Hampton, en Hampton
September New Hampshire Highland Games in Hopkinton	**Septiembre** Juegos Nuevo Hampshire Highland, en Hopkinton.
October Warner Fall Foliage Festival in Warner Pumpkin Festival in Keene	**Octubre** Festival del follaje otoñal de Warner, en Warner Festival de la calabaza, en Keene

New Hampshire Facts/
Datos sobre Nuevo Hampshire

Population
1.3 million

Población
1.3 millones

Capital
Concord

Capital
Concord

State Motto
Live Free or Die

Lema del estado
Vivir en libertad o morir

State Flower
Purple lilac

Flor del estado
Lila violeta

State Bird
Purple finch

Ave del estado
Pinzón morado

State Nickname
The Granite State

Mote del estado
Estado del Granito

State Tree
Paper birch

Árbol del estado
Abedul papelero

State Song
"Old New Hampshire"

Canción del estado
"Viejo Nuevo Hampshire"

State Gemstone
Smoky quartz

Piedra preciosa
Cuarzo ahumado

Famous New Hampshirites/
Neohampshireños famosos

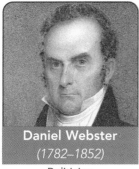
Daniel Webster
(1782–1852)

Politician
Político

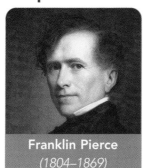
Franklin Pierce
(1804–1869)

U.S. president
Presidente de E.U.A

Sarah Josepha Hale
(1788–1879)

Author and journalist
Escritora y periodista

Horace Greely
(1811-1872)

Journalist
Periodista

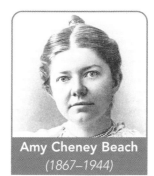
Amy Cheney Beach
(1867–1944)

Composer and pianist
Compositora y pianista

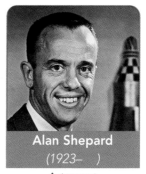
Alan Shepard
(1923–   )

Astronaut
Astronauta

Words to Know/Palabras que debes saber

border
frontera

granite
granito

outdoor
al aire libre

sculpture
escultura

Here are more books to read about New Hampshire:
Otros libros que puedes leer sobre Nuevo Hampshire:

In English/En inglés:

New Hampshire
By Brown, Dottie
First Avenue Editions, 2002

New Hampshire
By Wiener, Roberta and Arnold,
James R.
Raintree, 2004

Words in English: 390

Palabras en español: 402

Index

Índice